CW01425986

This notebook belongs to :

daddy André

Printed in Great Britain
by Amazon

53085917R00069